ATYS

Borgo Press Books Edited & Translated by FRANK J. MORLOCK

ATYS

A PLAY IN FIVE ACTS

by

Philippe Quinault

Translated and Adapted by Frank J. Morlock

THE BORGO PRESS

An Imprint of Wildside Press LLC

MMX

CONTENTS

DEDICATION

To

PAKO

(AKA)

FRANCISCO I. GARDUNO VELASCO

CAST OF CHARACTERS

THE TIMES

THE HOURS OF DAY AND NIGHT

THE GODDESS FLORA

A ZEPHYR

SERVANTS OF FLORA

FIGHTING AND DANCING HEROES

HERCULES

ATHENA

THE GODDESS IRIS

ATYS, relative of Sangaride and favorite of

Celenus, King of Phrygia

IDAS, Friend of Atys and brother of the nymph Doris

SANGARIDE, a nymph, daughter of the river Sangar

DORIS, a nymph, friend of Sangaride, and sister of Idas

CHORUS OF PHRYGIANS, (male and female)

TROUPE OF PHRYGIANS, (male and female who dance at the fest of Cybele)

THE GODDESS CYBELE

MELISSA, confidant and priestess of Cybele

TROUPE OF PRIESTESSES OF CYBELE

CELENUS, king of Phrygia, son of Neptune, and lover of Sangaride

TROUPE OF FOLLOWERS OF CELENUS

TROUPE OF ZEPHYRS, singing, dancing and flying

CHORUS OF DIFFERENT PEOPLE WHO COME TO THE FEST OF CYBELE

MORPHEUS, THE GOD OF SLEEP

PHOBETOR

PHANTASY

TROUPE OF AGREEABLE DREAMS

TROUPE OF HORRID DREAMS

THE GOD OF THE RIVER SANGAR, father of Sangaride

TROUPE OF RIVER AND STREAM GODS AND FOUNTAIN NYMPHS who sing and dance

ALECTO

TROUPE OF DIVINITIES OF WOODS AND STREAMS

TROUPE OF CORYBANTES

PROLOGUE

The stage represents the Palace of Time where this god appears in the midst of the twelve hours of the day and night.

TIME:

In vain, I've respected the celebrated memory
Of heroes of centuries past.
It's in vain that their names, so famous in history,
Have been bestowed widely.
We are looking at a hero whose brilliant glory
Has almost effaced all others.

CHORUS OF HOURS:

His just rule,
His great exploits,
Will render his memory eternal.
Each day, each moment,
Adds yet a new glory

To his dazzling name.

(The Goddess Flora led by a zephyr comes forward with a troupe of nymphs who wear diverse floral decorations.)

TIME:

Could frosty Winter offer us
The flowers that we see appear?
What god makes them reborn
After Fall makes them die?
Cruel cold reigns once more,
Everything in the fields is iced.
Where does Flora come from,
A step ahead of Spring?

FLORA:

If I wait for fine days, I always come too late;
The more Spring advances, the more it annoys me.
Its return presses the departure
Of heroes I wish to please.
To pay Spring my court my cares have undertaken,
Henceforth, to brave the most terrible winter.
In the ardor to please her, one soon learns
To find nothing impossible.

TIMES AND FLORA:

It's vain to present pleasures to his eyes.
No sooner does he see Bellona than he leaves for
her.
Nothing can stop him
When glory calls him.

(The Chorus of Hours repeats these two lines.)

(The followers of Flora begin to play games mixed
with dances and songs.)

A ZEPHYR:

Spring is sometimes less sweet than it seems.
It charges too much for its fine days.
It comes to dispel games and loves,
And it's Winter which brings them back together.

(Melpomene, the muse that presides over Tragedy,
enters accompanied by a troupe of heroes, she is
followed by Hercules, Anteus, Castor, and
Pollux, Lynceus, Etiocles and Polynices.)

MELPOMENE: (speaking to Flora)

Withdraw, cease to warn Time.
Don't rob me of precious moments.

The powerful Cybele
Has seized this day to honor Atys;
She wants me to revive
The memory of his love
In an illustrious court.
The rustic pleasure
Of Flora and these games
Give way to the magnificent display
Of the tragic muse
And her spectacular pomps.

(The suite of Melpomene takes the place of the suite of Flora.)

(The heroes resume their ancient quarrels. Hercules struggles with Anteus, Castor and Pollux against Lynceus and Idas, Etiocles against his brother Polynices.)

(Iris by the order of Cybele comes to conciliate Melpomene and Flora.)

IRIS: (speaking to Melpomene)

Cybele wants Flora to second you today.
Pleasures must come from every where
In the mighty empire where a new Mars reigns.
They have no other asylum in the world.
Make yourself, if you can, worthy of his notice.

Join pure and vivacious beauty
To whose glitter Nature
Adds ornaments of the most beautiful arts.

(The suite of Melpomene reconcile with Flora's
suite.)

MELPOMENE AND FLORA:
Let's make ourselves, if we can,
Worthy of his notice:
Let's join pure and vivacious beauty
To whose glitter Nature
Adds ornaments of the most beautiful arts.

TIME AND THE CHORUS OF HOURS:
Prepare new celebrations,
Let's prepare.
Profit from the leisure of the greatest of heroes.
Let's profit.

ALL TOGETHER:
The time of games and relaxation
Helps *him* meditate new conquests.

CURTAIN

ACT I

The action takes place in Phrygia.

The stage represents a mountain consecrated to Minerva.

ATYS:

Come on, get moving, everyone run.
Cybele is going to descend;
Most lucky Phrygians, come wait for her here.
Thousands of nations will be jealous
Of the favors that her bounty
Is going to shed over us.

IDAS (entering)

Come on, get moving, everyone run.
Cybele is going to descend.

ATYS:

The Sun paints our fields in the most vivid colors;

It has dried the tears
That dawn has shed over the gloss,
And its new rays have already made blossom
A thousand new flowers.

IDAS:

You watch when all sleep;
You awaken us in the mornings,
So that in the end you make us feel
That it's love that wakes you.

ATYS:

No! You must judge the role I take better;
My heart always wants to flee cares and mysteries.
I prefer the happy peace of indifferent hearts;
If their pleasures are not great,
At least their pains are slight.

IDAS:

Sooner or later love is conqueror.
In vain the most proud defy it.
You cannot refuse your heart
To the beautiful eyes that demand it.
Atys, feign no more, I know your secret.
Fear nothing, I am discreet.
In a solitary and somber woods,

The indifferent Atys thought himself alone one
day.
Under the thick foliage, where I was dreaming in
the shade.
I heard you speak of love.

ATYS:

If I speak of love, it's against its empire.
I make my sweetest conversation about it.

IDAS:

It's those whose hearts in secret sigh,
That boast of loving nothing.
I heard your complaints, and I know them so well
That if you doubt it, I am going to retell them to
you.
Lovers who pity, you are very lucky.
My heart—of all hearts—is the most loving
And very near expiring, I am reduced to pretending
That it's a rigorous torture
To die of love without complaining!
Lovers who pity, you are very lucky.

ATYS:

Idas, it's very true, my heart is just too tender.
Love makes me feel the most funereal blows

That no one but you can understand.

(Sangaride and Doris enter.)

SANGARIDE AND DORIS:
Come on, get moving, everybody run.
Cybele is going to descend.

SANGARIDE:
May her sacred name be heard
In our sweetest concerts.

ATYS:
Over the whole universe her power must extend.

SANGARIDE:
The gods follow her laws and fear her wrath.

ATYS, SANGARIDE, IDAS, AND DORIS:
What honors, what respect don't we owe her!
Come on, get moving, everybody run.
Cybele is going to descend.

SANGARIDE:

Listen to the birds of these surrounding woods.
They fill their songs with a new softness.
One would say, that on this fine day,
They are only speaking of Cybele!

ATYS:

If you listen to them they will speak of love;
A formidable king,
Amorous, amiable,
Is coming to be your spouse.
All speaks of love for you.

SANGARIDE:

It's true, I triumph and I love my victory.
Is there a greater benefit when love makes you reign?
For you, Atys, you love nothing,
And you glory in it.

ATYS:

Love makes too many tears shed.
Often its sweetness is mortal.
You must look at beauties
The way you do pretty flowers.
I love fresh roses.

I love to see them embellished.
Without their cruel thorns,
I would enjoy picking them

SANGARIDE:

When the peril is agreeable,
What's the use of being alarmed?
Is it a great sin to love too much
That which one finds lovable?
Can one be insensitive to the most charming attractions?

ATYS:

No, you don't know me;
I protect myself from loving as much as it's possible for me to do.
If, through misfortune, I were to love one day,
I know my heart too well,
It would be too sensitive.
But, it's necessary that each group around you;
Cybele might surprise us.

ATYS AND IDAS:

Come on, get moving, everybody run.
Cybele's going to descend.

(Exit Atys and Idas.)

SANGARIDE:

Atys is very happy.

DORIS:

Friendship was always the same between you two,
And blood links you closely.
Whatever may be his happiness, do you envy it,
You, who today must marry with such beautiful bonds
the King of Phrygia?

SANGARIDE:

Atys is very happy:
Sovereign of his heart, master of all his wishes,
Without fear, without melancholy,
He enjoys in relaxation the fine days of his life.
Atys doesn't experience the tortures of love.
Atys is very happy.

DORIS:

What wrong is love doing you?
Your pain astonishes me.

SANGARIDE:

I am confiding to you
A secret that is known to no one.
I ought to love a lover
Who offers me a crown.
But alas! duty
Vainly orders me to do it.
Love, for my torment,
Is ordering otherwise.

DORIS:

Would you love Atys, whose indifference
Braves love's power with so much pride?

SANGARIDE:

I love Atys in secret; my crime is unwitnessed.
To vanquish my love, I use every means.
I call on my reason, I animate my courage.
But what's the use of all my efforts?
My heart only suffers more,
And I don't love any less.

DORIS:

That's the common defect of beauties;
The passion of new conquests

Makes them neglect hearts that are too soon charmed,
And the indifferent are sometimes loved
At the expense of faithful lovers.
But you are exposing yourself to cruel pains.

SANGARIDE:

I will always be without attractions to Atys' eyes.
I know it, I consent to it. If possible, I wish
That he be even more insensitive.
If he could love me, what would become of me,
Alas!
It's my greatest good fortune that Atys doesn't love me.
I am pretending to be happy, at least in appearance;
I am going to attach myself to the destiny of a great king.

SANGARIDE:

An unfortunate love that offends duty
Must condemn itself in silence.
An unfortunate love that others can reproach us with
Knows only too well how to hide itself.

ATYS: (returning)

You can see in the fields
All our Phrygians advancing.

DORIS:

I am going to take pains to hurry
Our companions, the nymphs.

(Doris leaves.)

ATYS:

This day is a great day for you, Sangaride.

SANGARIDE:

The two of us are directing the feast of Cybele.
The honor is equal between us.

ATYS:

This very day a great king must be your spouse.
I've never seen you so happy and so beautiful
How sweet the fate of the king will be!

SANGARIDE:

The indifferent Atys won't be jealous.

ATYS:

The two of you will live happy, that's my dearest wish.
I have rushed your marriage, I have served your loves
But yet, this great day, the most beautiful of your life,
Will be the last day of mine.

SANGARIDE:

O gods!

ATYS:

It's only to you that I wish to reveal
The secret despair to which my misfortune delivers me.
I've only known how to pretend, it's time to speak.
He who has only a moment to live
No longer has anything to dissimulate.

SANGARIDE:

I shiver, my apprehension is extreme.
Atys, through what misfortune must I see you perish?

ATYS:

You will condemn me yourself,
And you will let me die.

SANGARIDE:

If necessary, I will enlist the supreme power—

ATYS:

No, nothing can help me
I am dying of love for you,
I don't know how to cure myself of it.

SANGARIDE:

What! You?

ATYS:

It's too true!

SANGARIDE:

You love me?

ATYS:

I love you.
You will condemn me yourself,

And you will let me die.
I deserve to be punished.
I am offending a generous rival
Who, by means of a thousand benefits, has fore-
seen my wishes.
But I offend him in vain; you will do him justice.
Ah! What a cruel torture this is,
To confess that a rival is worthy of being happy!
Pronounce my sentence! Speak without constraint.

SANGARIDE:

Alas!

ATYS:

You are sighing! I see your tears flow!
Do you pity the sorrows of a wretched love?

SANGARIDE:

Atys, how much you would complain
If you knew all your misfortunes!

ATYS:

If I am losing you, and if I am dying,
What more can I fear?

SANGARIDE:

Just of ruining me who charmed you,
You are ruining me, Atys, and you are loved.

ATYS:

Loved! What do I hear? O heaven! What a favorable admission.

SANGARIDE:

You will be more miserable for it.

ATYS:

My misfortune is more frightful.
The happiness that I am losing increases my rage.
But, no matter. If possible love me even more.
If I must die of it a hundred times more unhappy.

SANGARIDE:

If you seek death, I must follow you.
Live, it's my love which rules you.

ATYS:

Hey! What, hey! Why
Do you want me to live,

If you don't live for me?

ATYS AND SANGARIDE:

If marriage united my destiny and yours,
How attractive would have been its bonds.
Love makes our hearts one for each other.
Must duty separate them forever?

ATYS:

Pitiless duty!
Ah! What cruelty!

SANGARIDE:

Someone's coming; pretend once more, fear being
heard.

ATYS:

Let us love a bit longer
Like the dazzle of beauty,
Nothing is more pleasant
Than liberty.

(Enter Doris, Idas, and Choruses.)

ATYS:

Why, already from this sacred mount
The summit appears lit
With a new splendor.

SANGARIDE: (advancing towards the mountain)
The goddess is descending; let's go to meet her.

ATYS AND SANGARIDE:

Let's begin. Let's begin
To celebrate her solemn fest here.
Let's begin, let's begin
Our games and our songs.

(The Chorus repeats these last two lines.)

ATYS AND SANGARIDE:

It's time for each to let his zeal shine.
Come, Queen of Gods, come;
Come, favorable Cybele.

(The Chorus repeats the two last lines.)

ATYS:

Leave your immortal court.
Choose these fortunate parts
For your eternal dwelling.

THE CHORUSES:

Come, queen of gods, come.

SANGARIDE:

The earth under your feet is going to become more
beautiful
Like the dwelling of the gods you abandon.

CHORUSES:

Come, favorable Cybele.

ATYS AND SANGARIDE:

Come see the altars that are destined for you.

**ATYS, SANGARIDE, IDAS, DORIS AND THE
CHORUS**:

Hear a faithful people
Who are calling you.
Come, queen of gods, come.

Come, favorable Cybele.

(The Goddess Cybele appears and the Phrygians show her their joy and respect.)

CYBELE:
All come into my temple and let each revere
The priest I am going to choose.
I will explain through his voice.
The prayers that he will offer me will be sure to please me.
I receive your respect, I love to see the honors
With which you are presenting me a dazzling homage.
But the homage of hearts
Is what I love more.
You must animate yourselves
With a new ardor.
In order to honor Cybele
You must love her more.

(Cybele goes into her temple; all the Phrygians hurry to go with her, and repeat the last four verses spoken by the goddess.)

CHORUS:

We must animate ourselves
With a new ardor.
In order to honor Cybele
We must love her more.

CURTAIN

ACT II

The scene changes and represents the Temple of Cybele.

CELENUS:

Cybele is in these parts; don't follow my steps.
Leave. You, Atys, don't leave me.
We must wait for the goddess here
To name a high priest.

ATYS:

You will be her choice, Lord. What sorrow
Seems to have surprised your heart?

CELENUS:

The most mighty kings know the importance
Of a glorious choice
Which can extend his power
Everywhere that Cybele's laws are revered.

ATYS:

Today she honors these parts with her presence,
So as to prefer you to the most powerful kings.

CELENUS:

But when, just now, I saw the beauty who enchants
me,
Didn't you notice how she was trembling?

ATYS:

In our games, in our songs, I was too busy.
Outside the celebration, Lord, I noticed nothing.

CELENUS:

Her unease surprised me; she opens her soul to
you.
Could you discover there some secret flame,
Some hidden rival?

ATYS:

Lord, what are you saying?

CELENUS:

The mere name of rival excites my wrath.

I'm really afraid that heaven hasn't seen, without envy,
The happiness of my life.
And if I were loved, my fate would be too sweet.
Don't be so astonished to see the jealousy
With which my soul is seized.
You cannot love without being a bit jealous.

ATYS:

Lord, be content, let nothing alarm you.
Marriage is going to give you the beauty that charms you.
You will be her happy spouse.

CELENUS:

You are able to reassure me, Atys;
I want to believe you.
It's her heart that I want to have.
Tell me, is it in my power?

ATYS:

Her heart follows duty and glory with prudence.
And you have duty and glory on your side.

CELENUS:

Don't hide from me what you may know.
If I have what I love on this day,
Marriage alone will make me its master?
Glory and duty have everything, perhaps,
And are not leaving anything for me to love.

ATYS:

You love with a very tender, delicate love.

CELENUS:

The indifferent Atys is unable to understand it.

ATYS:

How lucky an indifferent person is!
He enjoys a peaceful destiny.
Heaven makes a very costly, very dangerous present
When it gives a heart too much sensitivity.

CELENUS:

When one loves really tenderly,
One never ceases to suffer and fear.
In the most charming happiness,
One is ingenious to discover a torture.

And one finds pleasure in pitying oneself.
Go, think of my marriage, and see if all is ready.
Leave me alone here, the goddess is appearing.

(Exit Atys. Enter Cybele, Melissa, and Cybele's Priestesses.)

CYBELE:

I want to unite glory and abundance in the parts:
I want to make the choice of a high-priest.
And the King of Phrygia must have the preference,
If I were to choose between the greatest kings.
The powerful god of the seas gave you birth;
A nation renowned is placed under your rule.
Without my help, you have besides, great power.
I wish to confer a blessing which is owed only to me.
You esteem Atys, and it's with justice
I pretend that my choice is propitious to your desires.
It's Atys I intend to choose.

CELENUS:

I love Atys, and I see his glory with pleasure.
I am king; Neptune is my father.
I am going to marry a beauty who is going to fulfill

my desires.
The wish remaining for me
Is to see my friend completely happy.

CYBELE:

It's delightful to me that my choice answers your wishes.
A great divinity
Must make her happiness
From the well being of all the world.
But especially the happiness of a king cherished by the heavens
Gives the greatest pleasure to the gods.

CELENUS:

Blood links Atys to the nymph that I love.
His merit equals that of kings.
He will support, better than I myself,
The supreme majesty
Of your divine laws.
Nothing can disturb his zeal.
His heart has been kept free until today.
Cybele must have a heart entirely.
Hardly all of mine could suffice to love her.

CYBELE:

Take the first news to your friend
Of the dazzling honor to which my favor calls him.

(Exit Celenus and his followers.)

CYBELE:

You are astonished, Melissa, and my choice surprises you!

MELISSA:

Atys owes you much and his happiness is great.

CYBELE:

I've done yet more for him than you can know.

MELISSA:

Is there a rank more glorious for a mortal?

CYBELE:

You only see his least glory.
This mortal in my heart is above the gods.
It was on the fatal day of my last fest
That I guessed the conquest of lovable Atys.

I left with regret to return to the heavens.
All seemed changed to me, nothing pleased my
sight.
I felt an extreme pleasure
To return to these parts.
Where can they ever be better
Then the place where one sees the one one loves?

MELISSA:

All the gods have loved; Cybele loves in her turn.
You used to scorn love too much.
Love's name seemed strange to you.
In the end there comes a day,
When love takes his revenge.

CYBELE:

I thought to make myself a heart
That was master of all its fate,
A heart forever free of tenderness and trouble.

MELISSA:

You wrongly braved
Love who wounds you.
The strongest heart
Has moments of weakness.
But you ought to be able to love and not descend so

far.

CYBELE:

No; too much equality renders love less attractive.
What higher rank have I to pretend to,
And what is there my power cannot bring about?
When one is above all,
One gives oneself pleasure to descend for love.
I am leaving to the gods the blessings prepared in heaven;
For Atys, for his heart, I am leaving it all without regret.
If he obliges me to descend, a sweet inclination drags me.
Hearts that destiny has separated the most
Are those that love unites with a very strong bond.
Make Sleep come: so that he himself, on this day,
May carefully escort here
Dreams which pay court.
Atys doesn't know my love.
Through a new means I pretend to instruct him of it.
(Melissa leaves to execute the orders of Cybele.)
Let the sweetest Zephyrs, let various peoples,
Who've come from the opposite ends of the universe
To demonstrate their zeal to me,

Celebrate the immortal glory
Of the high priest Cybele has chosen.
Atys must dispense my laws.
Honor the choice of Cybele.

(The Zephyrs appear in an elevated and shining glory. The various peoples who have come to the fest of Cybele enter the temple and all together endeavor to honor Atys, and greet him as the high priest of Cybele.)

CHORUS OF PEOPLES AND ZEPHYRS:
Let's celebrate the immortal glory
Of the high priest Cybele has chosen.
Atys must dispense her laws.
Let's honor the choice of Cybele.
May all before you abase themselves and tremble.
Live happily; your life is our hope;
Nothing is as beautiful to see joined together
Than great merit with great power.
May they bless her
Who, propitious heaven
Places in your hands
The fate of humans.

ATYS: (returning)

Unworthy though I am of the honors addressed me,
I must receive them in the name of the goddess.
I dare, because it pleases her, to present your
prayers to her.
As the reward of your zeal,
May mighty Cybele
Make you forever happy.

CHORUS OF PEOPLES AND ZEPHYRS:

May mighty Cybele
Make us forever happy.

CURTAIN

ACT III

The stage represents the palace of the high priest of Cybele.

ATYS: (alone)

What use are the favors that make our fortune,
When love makes us unhappy?
I am losing the blessing that can fulfill my desires,
And all other blessings annoy me.
What use are the favors that make our fortune,
When love makes us unhappy?

(Enter Idas and Doris.)

IDAS:

Can one speak openly here?

ATYS:

I command in these parts; you should fear nothing.

DORIS:

My brother is your friend.

IDAS:

Trust my sister.

ATYS:

You must share my good fortune with me.

IDAS AND DORIS:

We are coming to share our mortal alarms;
Sangaride, eyes in tears,
Has just revealed her heart to us.

ATYS:

The hour approaches when marriage wishes to con-
fide her
To the power of a lucky spouse.

IDAS AND DORIS:

She cannot live
For anyone but you.

ATYS:

Who can release her from the duty that presses her?

IDAS AND DORIS:

She wants to declare aloud,
At the feet of the goddess,
Your secret loves.

ATYS:

Cybele interests herself in me.
I dare to hope everything from her divine assis-
tance.
But what! To betray the king! To deceive his hope!
For so many benefits received, is this the reward?

IDAS AND DORIS:

In the empire of love,
Duty has no power.
Love relieves
Rivals of being generous.
They must often become happy
At the expense of a little innocence.

ATYS:

I wish, I fear, I want, I repent.

IDAS AND DORIS:

Will you see a rival happy at your expense?

ATYS:

I cannot decide on this violence.

ATYS, IDAS, AND DORIS:

In vain, a heart uncertain of its choice
Puts love and gratitude
In the balance. A thousand times
Love always outweighs the balance.

ATYS:

The most just partisan finally gives in to the
strongest.
Go, take care of my fate.
Let Sangaride present herself here in haste.

(Doris and Idas leave.)

ATYS: (alone)

We can flatter ourselves with the sweetest hope.
Cybele and Love are on our side,
But I hear the pressing voice of duty betrayed,
Which accuses me, and which shocks me.

Leave my heart in peace, powerless duty.
Haven't I struggled enough?
When Love, despite you, constrains me to surren-
der,
What are you asking of me?
Since you cannot protect me,
What use is it for me to listen
To the vain reproaches you are making?
Powerless virtue, leave my heart in peace.
May sleep come to surprise me.
I've vainly fought its charming sweetness.
It must suspend
The troubles of my heart.

(The set changes and represents a cavern sur-
rounded with poppies and streams where the God
of Sleep comes to relax, accompanied by pleasant
and frightening dreams. Atys is dozing.)

SLEEP:

Sleep, sleep everybody.
Ah, how sweet repose is!

MORPHEUS:

Reign, divine Sleep, reign over the whole world.
Spread your most soporific poppies,

Calm the cares, charm the senses,
Retain all hearts in a profound peace.

PHOBETOR:
Don't do yourself any violence;
Murmur, flow, clear streams,
Only a noise of water is permitted
To trouble the sweetness of such a charming si-
lence.

**SLEEP, MORPHEUS, PHOBETOR AND
PHANTASY**:

Sleep, sleep everybody.
Ah, how sweet repose is!

(Agreeable dreams approach Atys, and through
their songs and their dances acquaint him with the
love of Cybele and the happiness he must hope
for.)

MORPHEUS:
Listen, listen, Atys, glory is calling you.
Be sensitive to the honor of being loved by Cybele.
Rejoice, lucky Atys, in your blessing.

MORPHEUS, PHOBETOR AND PHANTASY:

But remember that beauty,
When it is immortal,
Demands the fidelity
Of an eternal love.

PHANTASY:

How love has attractions
When it begins
To make its power felt.
How love has attractions
When it begins
To never end!
Very happy the lover
That love exempts
From the pains of a long wait.
Very happy the lover
That love exempts
From fear and torment!

PHOBETOR:

Each day savor in peace a new delight.
Share the happiness coming from a divinity;
No longer boast of liberty,
It has no price compared to such a beautiful chain.

MORPHEUS, PHOBETOR AND PHANTASY:

But remember that beauty,
When it is immortal,
Demands the fidelity
Of an eternal love.

PHANTASY:

How love has attractions
When it begins
To make its power felt!
How love has attractions
When it begins
To never end!

(The funereal dreams approach Atys, they threaten him with the vengeance of Cybele if he scorns her love, and if he doesn't love her with fidelity.)

A FUNEREAL DREAM:

Beware of offending a glorious lover.
It's for you that Cybele is abandoning the heavens.
Don't betray her hopes,
The gods cannot be scorned innocently.
They have jealous hearts. They love vengeance.
It's dangerous to offend
An all-powerful love.

CHORUS OF FUNEREAL DREAMS:

Love that's outraged
Transforms itself into rage,
And never forgives
Even the most charming allures.
If you don't love Cybele,
Wretch! How you will suffer!
You will perish;
Fear a cruel vengeance;
Tremble, fear a frightful death.

(Atys, appalled by the funereal dreams, awakens with a start; Sleep and the Dreams vanish along with the cave from which they came, and Atys finds himself back in the palace where he had dozed off.)

ATYS:

Come to my aide, o gods! O just gods!

CYBELE:

Atys, fear nothing, Cybele is here.

ATYS:

Pardon the disorder in which my heart abandons

me.
It's a dream—

CYBELE:

Speak, what dream astonishes you?
Explain your distress to me.

ATYS:

Dreams are deceitful and I don't believe them.
Pleasures and pains
That one is seduced by when dozing,
Are vain chimeras
Which awakening destroys.

CYBELE:

Don't scorn dreams so much.
Love can borrow their voices.
If they often tell lies,
Sometimes they speak true.
They spoke at my command and you ought to believe them.

ATYS:

O heaven!

CYBELE:

Don't doubt it; know your glory,
Answer with freedom.
I'm asking of you a heart that depends on itself.

ATYS:

A great divinity
Must always be assured of my extreme respect.

CYBELE:

The gods, in their supreme grandeur,
Receive so many honors, that they are repelled by
'em.
They allow themselves to be respected too much.
They are more satisfied when they are loved.

ATYS:

I know too much what I owe you
To lack gratitude.

(Enter Sangaride, throwing herself at the feet of
Cybele.)

SANGARIDE:

I have recourse to your might;
Queen of gods, protect me.
The interest of Atys presses you concerning it—

ATYS: (interrupting Sangaride)

I will speak for you that your fear may cease.

SANGARIDE:

The two of us united by the most beautiful bonds—

ATYS: (interrupting Sangaride)

Blood and friendship unite us both.
May your aid deliver her
From the laws of a rigorous marriage.
The most sweet of her wishes
Is the ability to forever love and follow you.

CYBELE:

The gods are the protectors
Of hearts' liberty.
Go, do not fear the king or his wrath.
I will take care to appease
The river Sangar, your father.
Atys wants to favor you;

Cybele can refuse nothing in his favor.

ATYS:

Ah! That's too much—

CYBELE:

No, no; it is not necessary
That you hide your happiness.
I do not pretend to make
A vain mystery
Of a love that does you honor.
No need to fear saying too much to Cybele.
It is true, I love Atys; for him I've left everything.
Without him, I no longer want grandeur or sway.
For my happiness
His heart alone suffices.
(to Sangaride)
Go! Atys himself will go to guarantee you
From the fatal violence
To which you could not consent.
(Sangaride withdraws.)
(to Atys)
Leave us, carry out my orders for leaving;
I intend to arm you with my complete power.

(Atys and Sangaride leave.)

CYBELE:

How Atys mixed indifference with his respect!
The ingrate Atys doesn't love me.
Love demands love; all other rewards offend it.
And often, respect and gratitude
Are the excuse of ungrateful hearts.

MELISSA:

It's not such a great crime
Not to express oneself well.
A heart that's never loved anything
Doesn't know very well how to express itself.

CYBELE:

Sangaride is lovable, Atys can charm all;
They display too much esteem for each other,
And mere relatives are less in communication.
They've loved each other since childhood.
In the end they may love each other too much.
I fear a friendship animated by so much ardor.
Nothing is so deceitful as esteem.
It's a supposititious name
Sometimes given to love disguised.
I intend to enlighten myself; their trick will be use-
less.

MELISSA:

What secrets are not penetrated by the gods?
Two hearts preparing to feign
Vainly hide their chain.
They painfully abuse
The gods enlightened by love.

CYBELE:

Go, Melissa; give orders to the amiable Zephyr
To promptly accomplish all that Atys desires.

(Exit Melissa.)

CYBELE (alone)

Hope so dear and so sweet,
Ah! Why are you deceiving me?
You made me descend from supreme grandeurs.
Thousands of hearts adore me; I am neglecting
them all.
I demand only one; he has trouble to give himself.
And I experience the pain and suspicions of jeal-
ousy.
Is this the charming fate I ought to expect?
Hope so dear and so sweet
Ah! Why are you deceiving me?
Alas, with so many attractions could he fail to sur-

prise me!
Happy if always I had been able to protect myself!
Love which flattered me was hiding its wrath.
So it's left for me to strike the most funereal blows.
What cruel love has done to my tender heart!
Hope so dear and so sweet,
Ah! Why are you deceiving me?

CURTAIN

ACT IV

The set changes, and represents the Palace of the River Sangar.

DORIS:

What! You are crying!

IDAS:

Where does this mortal pain proceed from?

DORIS:

Didn't you dare to reveal your love to Cybele?

SANGARIDE:

Alas!

DORIS AND IDAS:

What can now increase your sorrows?

SANGARIDE:

Alas! I love—Alas! I love.

DORIS AND IDAS:

Get to the point.

SANGARIDE:

I cannot.

DORIS AND IDAS:

Love is not happy when it's timid.

SANGARIDE:

Alas! I love a perfidious liar
Who is betraying my love.
The goddess loves Atys; he's changed in less than
a day.
Atys, loaded down with honors no longer loves
Sangaride.
Alas, I love a perfidious liar
Who is betraying my love.

DORIS AND IDAS:

He demonstrated to us a little hesitation,

But who would have suspected him of so much in-
gratitude?

SANGARIDE:

I embarrassed Atys; I saw him so troubled.
I thought it my duty to reveal
Our love to Cybele.
But the ingrate, the false one
Kept preventing me from speaking.

DORIS AND IDAS:

Can one change so soon when love is intense?
Beware, beware
Of believing a jealous emotion too much.

SANGARIDE:

Cybele loudly declares that she loves him,
And the ingrate found this honor only too sweet.
He changed in a moment; I intend to change too.
I will accept a glorious spouse without trouble,
And I no longer want to love anything but supreme
grandeur.

DORIS AND IDAS:

Can one change so soon when love is intense?
Beware, beware
Of believing a jealous fit too much.

SANGARIDE:

Happy the heart that can believe
A scorn that serves its glory.
Return, my reason, return forever.
Join yourself to scorn to choke my flame.
Repair, if possible, the evils that Love has done me.
Come reestablish in my soul
The calms of happy peace.
Return, my reason, return forever.

IDAS AND DORIS:

A cruel infidelity
Doesn't efface all the charms
Of an unfaithful lover,
And reason doesn't return
As soon as it is called.

SANGARIDE:

After treachery,

If reason doesn't enlighten me,
Scorn and rage
Will keep me in place of reason.

SANGARIDE, DORIS AND IDAS:

How beautiful is the first flame!
How hard to break away from it!
How we must pity a faithful heart
When it is forced to change.

(Celenus and his suite enter.)

CELENUS:

Beautiful nymph, marriage is going to follow my
wish.
Love suits us,
And comes to place you on a dazzling throne.
I approach with delight this favorable moment
On which depends the happiness of the rest of my
life.
But despite the charms of happiness that awaits me,
Despite all the emotions of my amorous soul,
If I cannot make you happy,
I'll never be satisfied.
My happiness is to please you.
I attach my softest wishes to your heart.

SANGARIDE:

Lord, I will obey; I depend on my father,
And today my father wants me to be yours.

CELENUS:

Look on my love rather than on my crown.

SANGARIDE:

It's not grandeur that can dazzle.

CELENUS:

Could you love me without being directed to?

SANGARIDE:

Lord, content yourself that I know how to obey.
In the state I'm in, that's all I can say.

(Sangaride notices Atys enter.)

CELENUS:

Your heart's troubled, it sighs.

SANGARIDE:

Explain in your favor
Whatever you see of unease in my heart.

CELENUS:

Nothing alarms me any more! Atys, my fear is idle.
At last my love touches the heart of the beauty,
With whom I am enchanted.
You, who were witness to my pain,
Dear Atys, be witness to my happiness.
Can you conceive it? No, you have to love her
To judge the gladness of my extreme happiness.
But, close to seeing the fulfillment of my wishes,
How long the moments are to my amorous heart.
Your relatives are too slow; I intend to go myself
To hurry them to make me happy.

(Exit all but Atys and Sangaride.)

ATYS:

How little he knows his misfortune! And how de-
plorable that is!
His love deserves a more favorable fate.
I pity the error in which his heart is flattering itself.

SANGARIDE:

Spare yourself the trouble of being so compassion-
ate;
His love will obtain what it deserves.

ATYS:

Gods! What's this I hear?

SANGARIDE:

I have to revenge myself;
So finally I will love the king when he becomes my
spouse.

ATYS:

Sangaride! Hey! What causes this strange change?

SANGARIDE:

Isn't it you, ingrate, who want me to change?

ATYS:

Me!

SANGARIDE:

What treachery!

ATYS:

What funereal wrath!

ATYS AND SANGARIDE:

Why abandon myself to a new passion?
It's not I who am breaking such a beautiful bond.

ATYS:

Too cruel beauty, it is you.

SANGARIDE:

Faithless lover, it is you.

ATYS:

Ah! It is you, cruel beauty.

SANGARIDE:

No! It's you, faithless lover!

ATYS AND SANGARIDE:

Too cruel beauty, it is you.
Faithless lover it is you,
Who breaks such sweet bonds.

SANGARIDE:

You have sacrificed me on the altar of Cybele.

ATYS:

It's true that before her eyes, from a secret terror,
I wanted our hearts to hide their understanding.
But it's only for you that I fear her vengeance,
And I have no fear for myself.
Cybele loves me vainly and it's you that I adore.

SANGARIDE:

After your infidelity
Could you really be so cruel
As to want to deceive me again?

ATYS:

Me, betray you! You think that!
Ingrate! How you offend me!
Well! There's no longer need to be silent.
I am going to the goddess to stir up her rage
To offer myself to her fury since you force me to it.

SANGARIDE:

Ah! Remain, Atys. My suspicions are over.
You love me, I know it, I wanted to be certain of it.

I wish it enough
To believe it without pain.

ATYS:

I swear.

SANGARIDE:

I promise.

ATYS AND SANGARIDE:

To never change.

SANGARIDE:

What torture to hide such a beautiful flame.

ATYS:

Let's redouble the passion in the depth of our soul.

ATYS AND SANGARIDE:

Let's love in secret; let's love each other
Let's love more than ever, despite jealousy.

SANGARIDE:

My father is here.

ATYS:

Let nothing astonish you.
Let's use the power that Cybele is giving me;
I am going to prepare the Zephyrs
To follow our wishes.

(Exit Atys. From another direction enter Celenus,
The God of the River Sangar, a troupe of River
Gods, of Streams and Fountains.)

THE GOD OF THE RIVER SANGAR:

O you who share in the happiness of my family,
You venerable gods of the greatest rivers.
My faithful friends and most dear relations,
See the spouse to whom I am giving my daughter.
I've taken care to choose from the greatest kings.

CHORUS OF RIVER GODS:

We approve your choice.

THE GOD OF THE RIVER SANGAR:

He had Neptune for his father,

He rules the Phrygians.
I thought I lacked the power
To make a choice more worthy of pleasing you.

CHORUS OF RIVER GODS:

All of us with a common voice.
We approve your choice.

THE GOD OF THE RIVER SANGAR:

Let them sing, let them dance.
Let's all laugh, since we must.
It's never too soon
For pleasure to begin.
The end comes soon enough
To days of rejoicing.
It's useless to chase away pain,
It returns before you can think of it.

**THE GOD OF THE RIVER SANGAR AND
THE CHORUS**:

Let them sing, let them dance.
Let's all laugh since we must.
It's never too soon
For pleasure to begin.
Let them sing, let them dance.

Let's all laugh, since we must.

GODS OF RIVERS, DIVINITIES OF FOUNTAINS AND STREAMS, SINGING AND DANCING TOGETHER:

The most strict beauty
Takes pity on a long torment
And the lover who perseveres
Becomes a happy lover.
All is sweet and costs nothing
For a heart one wishes to touch.
The ocean makes a route,
And by force of seeking it,
Water falling drop by drop
Pierces the hardest rock.
Marriage alone doesn't know how to please.
It's vain to flatter our wishes;
Love alone has the right to tie
The sweetest of all bonds.
He's proud; he's rebellious,
But he charms, such as he is.
Marriage comes when called
Love comes when it pleases.
There's no resisting
When the time comes in the end
And the strength of constancy
Finally must conquer all.

All is sweet and costs nothing
To a heart one wishes to touch.
The ocean makes a route,
And by force of seeking it,
Water falling drop by drop
Pierces the hardest rock.
Love bothers everybody.
It's the source of our tears;
It's a raging fire in the ocean;
It's the stumbling block of great hearts.
It's proud, it's rebellious,
But it charms, such as it is.
Marriage comes when called,
Love comes when it pleases.

**A RIVER GOD AND A FOUNTAIN DIVIN-
ITY, DANCING AND SINGING TOGETHER**:

With extreme constancy
A stream runs its course.
It will be the same
With the choice of my amours.
And from the moment that I love
It will be to love forever.
Never a flighty heart
Will find a happy fate.
There's no future

In being a long while in port.
It seeks the storm again
At the moment it leaves.

CHORUS OF RIVER GODS AND FOUNTAIN DIVINITIES:

A great calm is very annoying,
We prefer torture.
What use is a heart that exemplifies
All the virtues of love?
What use is dormant water?
A great calm is very annoying,
We prefer torture.

(Atys and Celenus enter.)

CHORUS OF GODS OF RIVERS AND FOUNTAINS:

Come form charming fetters,
Atys, come unite these happy lovers.

ATYS:

The marriage displeases Cybele.
She forbids it to be consummated.
Sangaride is a blessing she must reserve for herself.
And that I demand for her.

THE CHORUS:

Ah! What a cruel decision!

CELENUS:

Atys is able to engage himself to betray me!
Atys interests himself against me!

ATYS:

Lord, I belong to the goddess;
When she commands, I can only obey.

THE GOD OF THE RIVER SANGAR:

Why must she separate
Two illustrious lovers for whom marriage is pre-
paring
The softest of bonds?

CHORUS:

Let's oppose
This barbarous plan.

ATYS:

Know, audacious ones,
That there is nothing but to obey

The sovereign laws of the Queen of the Gods!
Let us be carried away from these parts.
Zephyrs, accomplish my orders without delay.

(The Zephyrs carry off Atys and Sangaride.)

CHORUS:
What injustice!

CURTAIN

ACT V

The scene represents agreeable gardens.

CELENUS:

Inhuman, Cybele! You take Sangaride away from me!
Is this the reward of zeal,
I have performed carefully to dazzle your eyes?
Are you preparing yourself in this way the eternal sweetness
With which you must crown these parts?
Is this the way that kings are protected by the gods?
Cruel divinity,
Are you coming down from the heavens
To trouble a faithful love?
And coming to take from me what I love best?

CYBELE:

I loved Atys; love made my injustice.
It has taken care of my punishment
And, if you were outraged,
Soon you will be very well avenged.
Atys adores Sangaride.

CELENUS:

Atys adores her! Ah! The perfidious one!

CYBELE:

The ingrate betrayed you, and wants to betray me;
He's deceived himself in thinking to blind me.
The zephyrs have left him alone with the one he loves
In these lovely parts
I am hiding myself from their eyes,
I've just been witness to their intense love.

CELENUS:

O heaven! Atys will please the eyes that have charmed me!

CYBELE:

Hey! Can you suspect that Atys will not be loved?

No, no; never has love had so much violence.
They have sworn a hundred times to love each
other despite us,
And to brave all our vengeance.
They have called us tyrants, jealous ones
Finally, their hearts communicate,
the two of them—ah! I shiver at the moment I
think of it!
The two of them abandoning themselves to such
sweet distractions—
That I have been unable to keep silent any longer
Nor to restrain the outburst of my just wrath.

CELENUS:

For their crime death is a mild punishment.

CYBELE:

My heart is sufficiently engaged to punish them.
I already told you; trust in my wrath.
Soon you will be very well avenged.

(Enter Atys, Sangaride, Melissa, and a troupe of
Cybele's priestesses.)

CYBELE AND CELENUS:

You are coming to deliver yourself to death.

ATYS AND SANGARIDE:

What! Heaven and earth are armed against us!
Will you tolerate their punishing us?

CYBELE AND CELENUS:

Have you forgotten your injustice?

ATYS AND SANGARIDE:

Can't you recollect having loved us?

CYBELE AND CELENUS:

You are changing my love into legitimate hate.

ATYS AND SANGARIDE:

Can you condemn us
For the love which animates us?
If it's a crime
What crime is more pardonable?

CYBELE AND CELENUS:

Perfidious ones! You owe it to me to shut up.

How vainly I wanted to please you!

ATYS AND SANGARIDE:

Unable to follow your wishes,
We thought we could do no better
Than spare you mortal displeasure.

CYBELE:

Fear the intense horror of a cruel death.

CYBELE AND CELENUS:

Fear a funereal execution.

ATYS AND SANGARIDE:

Avenge yourselves if you must; don't pardon me,
But pardon the one I love.

CYBELE AND CELENUS:

Betraying us isn't enough,
You brave us, too, ingrates.

ATYS AND SANGARIDE:

Will you be without pity?

CYBELE AND CELENUS:

Abandon all hope.

ATYS AND SANGARIDE:

Love forced us to offend you,
It demands mercy for us.

CYBELE AND CELENUS:

Love in wrath
Demands vengeance.

CYBELE:

You who bring rage and horror everywhere,
Cease to torture criminal shades.
Come, cruel Alecto, leave your somber realms,
Inspire the heart of Atys with your barbaric furor.

(Alecto enters, along with Idas and Doris, and the
Phrygian chorus. Alecto leaves hell, holding a
torch in her hand which she shakes over the head
of Atys.)

ATYS:

Heaven! What vapor surrounds me!
All my senses are troubled, I shake, I shiver,

I tremble, and suddenly an infernal passion
Comes to inflame my blood, and devour my heart.
Gods! What do I see? Heaven is arming itself
against the earth!
What disorders! What uproars! What bursts of
thunder!
What profound abysses are opening beneath my
feet!
What vain ghosts are coming out of hell!

(speaking to Cybele whom he takes for Sangaride)

Sangaride, ah! Flee the death prepared for you
By a barbarous divinity.
It's your peril alone which causes my terror.

SANGARIDE:

Atys, recognize your funereal error.

ATYS: (taking Sangaride for a monster)

What monster comes to us!
What furor guides him!
Ah! Cruel thing, respect the loveable Sangaride.

SANGARIDE:

Atys, my dear Atys.

ATYS:

What horrifying howling!

CELENUS: (to Sangaride)

Flee, escape from his rage.

ATYS: (holding in his hand the sacred knife which is used for sacrifices)

Got to fight; love, second my courage.

(Atys runs after Sangaride, who flees into the wings.)

CELENUS AND THE CHORUS:

Stop, stop, wretch!

(Celenus runs after Atys.)

SANGARIDE: (off)

Atys!

CHORUS:

O heaven!

SANGARIDE:

I am dying.

CHORUS:

Atys, Atys himself
Is causing the one he loves to perish!

CELENUS: (returning to the stage)

I could not restrain his furious strength.
Sangaride is expiring before your eyes.

CYBELE:

Atys was sacrificing me to an unworthy rival
Share with me the unequaled delight
That one tastes in avenging an outraged love.
I promised it to you.

CELENUS:

O fatal promise!
Sangaride is no more, and
I am too well avenged.

(Celenus retires to the side of the stage where Sangaride lies dead.)

ATYS: (returning)

How I've just sacrificed a great victim!
Sangaride is saved, and it's through my valor.

CYBELE: (touching Atys)

Complete my vengeance; Atys, learn your crime
And resume your reason to feel your misfortune.

ATYS:

A happy calm succeeds the troubles of my heart.
Sangaride, charming nymph,
What's become of you? Where can I have recourse?
All mighty divinity
Cybele, have pity on our tender loves,
Return Sangaride to me, spare her beautiful life.

CYBELE: (pointing to the dead Sangaride)

You can see her; look.

ATYS:

Ah! What barbarism!

Sangaride has lost her life.
Ah! What cruel hand! Ah! What inhuman heart!

CYBELE:

The blows that killed her are from your own hand.

ATYS:

Me, I could have sacrificed the beauty that enchants me!
O heaven! My bloody hand
Is too certain a witness to this horrible crime!

CHORUS:

Atys himself
Caused the one he loves to perish.

ATYS:

What! Sangaride is dead! Atys is her executioner!
What vengeance, o gods! What new torture!
What horrors are comparable
To the horrors I feel?
Cruel gods, pitiless gods!
Are you all-mighty
Only for making misery?

CYBELE:

Atys, I loved you too much.
That love, was transformed to wrath by you your-
self.
Look at its violence again.
Judge, ingrate, judge, on this funereal day,
Of the grandeur of my love
By the grandeur of my vengeance.

ATYS: Barbarian!

Some love that takes care to invent
The most horrible ills that rage can devise!
Happy those who can avoid
The misfortune of pleasing you.
O gods! Unjust gods! Why aren't you mortal!
Why must it be for you alone to own vengeance?
It's too much, it's too much to suffer their cruel
power.
Let's chase them out of here, overthrow their al-
tars.
What! Sangaride is dead! Atys, Atys himself
Caused what he loved to perish!

CHORUS:

Atys, Atys himself
Caused what he loved to perish.

CYBELE (ordering them to take away the body of Sangaride)

Remove this sad object.

ATYS:

Ah! Don't tear from me
What remains of so much charm.
And to make you jealous again
I must adore her,
Even in the horror of death.

(Exit Atys after the corpse with all the others, leaving Cybele and Melissa alone.)

CYBELE:

I am beginning to find his pain very cruel.
A tender pity,
A tender pity recalls the
The love that my wrath thought it had banished.
My rival is no more. Atys is no longer guilty.
How easy it is to love an attractive criminal.
After having punished him.
How his despair dismays me!
His life is in peril, and I shiver with fright
I wish with a care so dear not to trust anyone except myself.

Let's go— But what spectacle is presenting itself
to my eyes?
It's Atys dying that I see.

(Enter Atys, Idas, and the priestesses of Cybele.)

IDAS: (supporting Atys)

He's pierced his breast
And my cares for his life
Were not able to forestall his fury.

CYBELE:

Ah! This is my barbarism,
It's I who pierced his heart

ATYS:

I am dying; love is guiding me
Through the night of death.
I am going where Sangaride will be.
Inhuman! I am going where you won't be.

CYBELE:

Atys, it's too true, my harshness was extreme.
Complain, I want to suffer everything.
Why am I immortal when I am watching you per-

ish?

ATYS AND CYBELE:

It is sweet to die
With the one one loves.

CYBELE:

Why can't my funereal love, armed against itself,
Avenge you against all my harshness?

ATYS:

I am sufficiently avenged; you love me and I am
dying.

CYBELE:

Despite the implacable destiny
That renders an irrevocable decree with your death,
Atys, be forever the object of my love.
Resume a new fate, become a lovely tree
That Cybele will always love.

(Atys takes the form of the tree beloved of the
Goddess Cybele, called the pine.)

CYBELE:

Come, furious corybantes,
Come join with my screams your furious clamors.
Come water nymphs, come forest deities.
With your most touching wails
Second my sad regrets.

(Enter a troupe of water nymphs, woodland deities, and corybantes.)

CYBELE:

Atys, lovable Atys with all his charms
Is descending into eternal night.
But, despite cruel death,
The love of Cybele
Will never die.
Under a new shape
Atys is revived by my divine power.
Celebrate his new destiny.
Cry for his funereal mischance.

CHORUS OF WATER NYMPHS AND FOR- EST DEITIES:

Let's celebrate his new destiny.
We are crying for his funereal mischance.

CYBELE:

Let this sacred tree
Be revered
By all nature.
Let it be raised above the most beautiful trees.
Let it be neighbor to the heavens, let it reign over
the waters,
Let it burn only with a pure flame.
Let this sacred tree
Be revered
By all nature.

(The Chorus repeats the last three verses.)

CYBELE:

May its branches be ever green.
May the harshest winters
Never injure them.
Let this sacred tree
Be revered by all nature.

(The Chorus repeats these last three verses.)

CYBELE AND THE CHORUS OF WOOD-LAND DIVINITIES AND WATER NYMPHS:

What sorrow!

CYBELE AND THE CHORUS OF CORY-BANTES:

Ah! What rage!

CYBELE AND THE CHORUSES:

Ah, what misfortune!

CYBELE:

Atys, in the springtime of his age,
Perished like a flower
That a sudden storm
Overturns and ravages.

CYBELE AND THE CHORUS OF WOOD-LAND DEITIES AND WATER NYMPHS:

What sorrow!

CYBELE AND THE CHORUS OF CORY-BANTES:

Ah! What rage!

CYBELE AND ALL THE CHORUSES:

Ah! What misfortune!

(The woodland divinities and the water nymphs together with the Corybantes honor the new tree, and consecrate it to Cybele. Their regrets are seconded and terminated by a trembling of the earth, by lightning flashes and thunder.)

CYBELE AND THE CHORUS OF WOODLAND DEITIES AND WATER NYMPHS:

How the misfortune of Atys afflicts all the world.

CYBELE AND THE CHORUS OF CORYBANTES:

Let everything around here feel
The horror of such a cruel death.

CYBELE AND THE CHORUS OF WOODLAND DEITIES AND WATER NYMPHS:

Let's penetrate hearts with a profound sorrow.
Let woods, let waters lose their attractions

CYBELE AND THE CHORUS OF CORY-BANTES:

Let thunder answer us.
Let the earth tremble and shake under our feet.

CYBELE AND THE CHORUS OF WOOD-LAND DEITIES AND WATER NYMPHS:

Let the misfortune of Atys afflict the whole world.

ALL TOGETHER:

Let everything around here feel
The horror of such a cruel death.

CURTAIN

ABOUT FRANK J. MORLOCK

FRANK J. MORLOCK has written and translated many plays since retiring from the legal profession in 1992. His translations have also appeared on Project Gutenberg, the Alexandre Dumas Père web page, Literature in the Age of Napoléon, Infinite Artistries.com, and Munsey's (formerly Black-mask). In 2006 he received an award from the North American Jules Verne Society for his translations of Verne's plays. He lives and works in México.

www.ingramcontent.com/pod-product-compliance
Lightning Source LLC
LaVergne TN
LVHW011213080426
835508LV00007B/756